land of the far horizon

a guide to
Northumberland
National Park

foreword

Tides of history, the hopes and dreams of empires and kings, have ebbed and flowed across the Borderlands. So have the lives of shepherds and labourers.

What is now defined as Northumberland National Park is the gathering of elements, ribbons of moorland, cascades of water and the bleached quilt of the border hills. It is landscape on a grand scale, something unusual in our crowded island; it fills the senses and feeds the imagination.

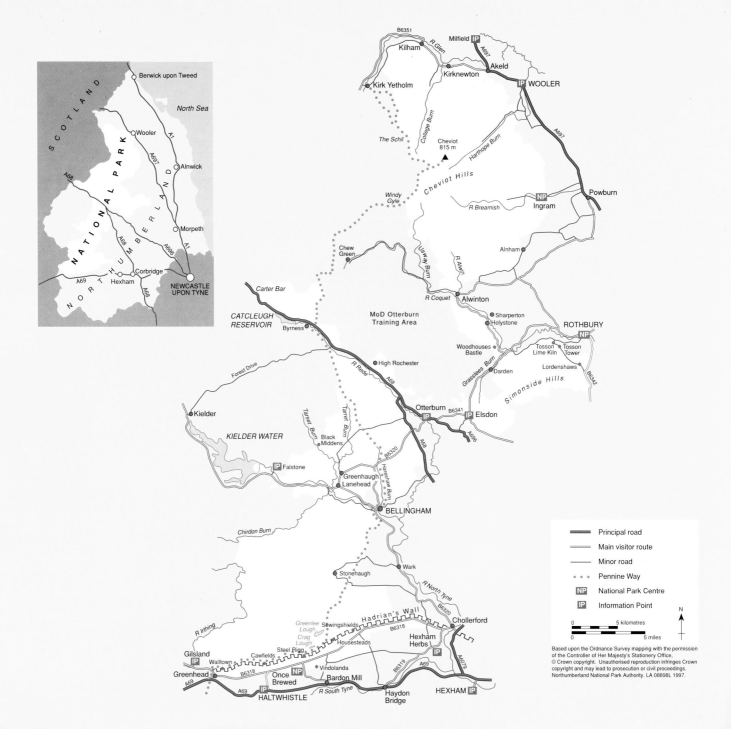

SCOTLAND

North Sea

NATIONAL PARK

NORTHUMBERLAND

Berwick upon Tweed

Wooler

Alnwick

Morpeth

Corbridge
Hexham

NEWCASTLE UPON TYNE

A1
A697
A68
A696
A69

B6351
Kilham
R Glen
Milfield **IP**
Akeld
Kirknewton
IP WOOLER
A697

Kirk Yetholm

The Schil

Cheviot
815 m

Cheviot Hills
Harthope Burn

Windy Gyle

R Breamish
NP
Ingram
Powburn

Chew Green

Usway Burn
R Alwin

Alnham

Carter Bar

CATCLEUGH RESERVOIR
Byrness

MoD Otterburn Training Area

R Coquet
Alwinton

Sharperton
Holystone
ROTHBURY
NP

Forest Drive

R Rede
High Rochester
A68

Woodhouses Bastle
Grasslees Burn
Darden
Tosson Lime Kiln
Tosson Tower
Lordenshaws
B6342

Simonside Hills

Kielder

KIELDER WATER

Tarset Burn
Tarret Burn
Black Middens

Otterburn
IP
B6341
IP Elsdon
A68
A696

IP Falstone

Greenhaugh
Lanehead

B6320
Hareshaw Burn

BELLINGHAM

Chirdon Burn

Stonehaugh
Wark

R North Tyne
B6320

Greenlee Lough
Sewingshields
Hadrian's Wall
Chollerford
Crag Lough
B6318
Housesteads
Hexham Herbs
IP

Gilsland
IP
Walltown
Cawfields
Steel Rigg
B6318
Once Brewed **NP**
Vindolanda
Bardon Mill
B6319
A69
A6079

Greenhead
A69
HALTWHISTLE
R South Tyne
Haydon Bridge
HEXHAM **IP**

R Irthing

	Principal road
	Main visitor route
	Minor road
••••	Pennine Way
NP	National Park Centre
IP	Information Point

0   5 kilometres
0   5 miles

N

first impressions

National Parks were created to conserve the finest landscapes of England and Wales and to encourage people to enjoy and appreciate their special qualities. One of eleven National Parks, Northumberland was designated in 1956 and covers nearly four hundred square miles, stretching from Hadrian's Wall World Heritage Site in the south to the Cheviot Hills in the north. The look of the land and the use to which it has been put depends on bedrock and climate, and centuries of farming experience. Most of the remote uplands are open pasture, usually composed of tussocky mat-grass, or heather where the moors are managed for grouse.

Northumberland National Park is an area of great natural beauty and historic interest. This guide illustrates some of the many places worth visiting in England's most northerly National Park.

Perhaps the most memorable aspect of the Northumberland hills is the sense of open space, of being away from everything and everybody. This is partly due to the scarcity of roads and the lack of any major towns, and partly the result of long-forgotten wars, when the land was laid waste and neither houses nor trees were left standing. By the time the Borders were safe, the Industrial Revolution was under way and people were attracted into towns and away from the land. Over the past few decades even some of the tenant farmers have moved further down the valleys, leaving the hills to hardy sheep and shepherds.

Bad weather days on the Cheviot and Simonside Hills or the switch-back ridge of Hadrian's Wall can be daunting, but the good days are wonderful. Old drove roads and sheep paths on firm turf make hill walking a pleasure. The sky becomes an important feature of landscape. The nineteenth century historian Trevelyan called Northumberland 'land of the far horizon' and it is possible to walk for a whole day without seeing a living soul.

park profile

- The Park has the cleanest and purest rivers, burns and lakes in England.

- Over 2,000 species of animals and plants are known in the Park and the list is growing all the time.

- 10% of the Park is designated as a Site of Special Scientific Interest.

- 66% of the Park is classified as moorland, 20% is coniferous forest, 5% peatland (blanket bogs and mires) and less than 1% is semi-natural woodland.

- There are 200 listed buildings in the Park, 250 Scheduled Ancient Monuments and a World Heritage Site, Hadrian's Wall.

- The Park comprises 230 farms, 35 Sites of Special Scientific Interest, 56 Sites of Nature Conservation Importance and three National Nature Reserves.

- There are 414kms (257 miles) of public footpaths and 168kms (104 miles) of bridleway and 50kms (31 miles) of byeways in the Park.

- Only 0.2% of the land is owned by the Park Authority. 54% is in private ownership, 23.1% is owned by the Ministry of Defence, 18.9% by Forest Enterprise, 2.4% by Water Companies and 1.1% by the National Trust.

wall country

Without its spectacular setting Hadrian's Wall would not be half so impressive or exciting. But when the Romans built the Wall, in about 122 AD, they chose to run their ultimate deterrent along the crest of the Whin Sill, one of the most important geological features in North East England. The Whin Sill is an intrusion of hard volcanic rock called dolerite. It appears in Northumberland as a broken ridge with a steep north-facing scarp slope of crags and scree. The military zone which marked the north west frontier of the Roman Empire stretched across Britain from sea to sea. It consisted of a Wall, ditch, forts, milecastles (Cawfields, bottom right), turrets and roads, with right of passage north and south for civilians at specified crossing points. The vallum, a great earthwork the equivalent of the Berlin Wall, marked the southern boundary of the military zone. So there was more to the edge of empire than a big wall and there are more archaeological sites here to tell the tale, such as the forts at Chesters, Housesteads and Vindolanda, than in any comparable section of countryside in the whole of Britain.

The most famous remains of the Wall run through the National Park between the River Irthing and the North Tyne. Visitors are sometimes surprised to find that for long intervals there are only grass-covered mounds to mark the line of the Wall. For centuries it provided a convenient source of ready-dressed stone. Today, more of Hadrian's Wall is found in barns, farmhouses and field walls than on its original foundations, but there are some fine surviving stretches.

The Whin Sill not only bears the ruins of the Wall, it also provides an assortment of wildlife habitats including rocky outcrops and grassland, where rock-rose and wild chive are found. Shallow lakes (loughs), such as Crag Lough and Greenlee Lough, are an important winter refuge for wildfowl including whooper swans and greylag geese. The area is also notable for birds of prey like peregrine and merlin.

The most spectacular section on the Wall is between Walltown and Sewingshields. Access by public transport or car is from car parks signed off the B6318 at Walltown, Cawfields, Steel Rigg and Housesteads. There are toilets and attractive picnic sites at both Walltown and Cawfields.

into the mire

Centuries ago there were extensive mires over most of upland Britain. All but a few fragments have been drained and some of the best of these are in Northumberland National Park in the area north of Hadrian's Wall.

During the Anglo-Scottish wars (1296–1603) the most daunting obstacles to cross-border raids were mires rather than mountains. Peat bogs earned a grim reputation as places to be avoided, though Reivers (thieves) and drovers knew secret ways. Today, bogs inspire curiosity rather than fear. They can be very beautiful places, alive, full of colour and decked by some of the most exquisite wild flowers.

Bogs thrive on rain and on being left alone. The few hundred years after the last Ice Age were important; soil nutrients were used up and rainfall got heavier. Wet scrapes in the bedrock were filled by bog-moss and layer grew over layer until great domes had been created, defying gravity like a series of sodden sponges. Beneath the living bog-moss lay lozenges of peat up to 10,000 years old and over the surfaces spread traceries of flowers.

In Northumberland most of the finest mires such as Greenlee, Hangingshields Rigg, The Wou and Felicia Moss are protected as Nature Reserves. The plant communities vary from place to place but usually include bog asphodel and sundew (left), cranberry and bog rosemary. Greenlee is so important that it is designated as a National Nature Reserve. A leaflet available from the National Park Centre at Once Brewed describes how to get there and what to see from the bird hide and from the boardwalk across the mire.

The Large Heath Butterfly
The large heath butterfly is only found on northern bogs and is a speciality of the National Park. The small circle on the butterfly's wing tip is a false eye-spot. Meadow pipits and other predators peck at the wrong end of the butterfly, allowing it time to escape.

Coquetdale

Most people know that the uplands of Britain were once covered with ice and that glaciers bludgeoned out the valleys and smoothed the mountains' contours.

But it is hard to stand in the countryside and imagine how it looked thousands of years ago. Winter in parts of Upper Coquetdale comes close to the vision of post-glacial Britain; a broad, gravel-lined valley with close-shaven slopes and hardly a tree to break the skyline. Caribou might look at home here.

The valleys that radiate from the high Cheviots all have this virginal look, as if they have been by-passed by human influence. But it is just an illusion. All the valleys have been cleared of their natural cover and farmed for at least a hundred generations.

The River Coquet rises on the Border Ridge and on its journey through the National Park it evolves from a peaty cleft to a tumbling burn, then to a stony stream and finally to a meandering river, as shown left, near Harehaugh. Over the centuries its pastures and sheltered terraces have attracted farms and scattered hamlets and villages. In Norman times the de Umfraville family built an imposing castle to guard the dale at Harbottle; the motte-hill and fragments of the walls can be seen from the road west of the village. Further down the valley lies Holystone, with its holy well dedicated to St Ninian, and Woodhouses Bastle, a defensible farmhouse dating from the 16th century. Outside the National Park, but in the shadow of the Simonside Hills, lies the little town of Rothbury. It acts as a gateway to Coquetdale and houses a National Park Centre.

The Coquet is reputed to be one of the best salmon and trout rivers in Britain. In the upper reaches small fish, often no bigger than minnows, provide rich pickings for dippers, herons and goosanders.

Woodhouses (NT 967003) is probably the best preserved bastle in the National Park. Access to this historic building, set in attractive parkland, is via a permissive path from a layby on the unclassified road to Holystone and Harbottle, and about one mile from Sharperton on the B6341.

homes in the hills

Settlements are few and far between in the National Park. The boundary was drawn deliberately to include the high hills and exclude small market towns such as Rothbury, Wooler, Bellingham and Hexham. Within the arc created by these communities lie a few villages or hamlets, scattered around levelled ground in the foothills or along broadening valleys. Often these villages date back at least to medieval times, the houses sometimes grouped around a green and a small church. Because of the insecurity of the Border and the poverty of the people, most of the early dwellings were ramshackle structures, easy to burn down and to rebuild. Thus, the oldest surviving buildings are the churches, (such as Alnham below) usually resting on Saxon or Norman foundations, and the castles, towers and bastles, defensible dwellings of powerful families and yeomen farmers.

In the 18th and 19th centuries, when the Borders were finally at peace, solid stone houses appeared and it is these that give the villages their present character. In the villages of the National Park there is an independence bred of isolation, of having to cope with hard living conditions. However, these days families in remote settlements cannot survive without their own transport. They shop and send their children to school in the local market towns and travel further afield to major shopping centres on Tyneside and to support Newcastle United.

Falstone, Elsdon, Stonehaugh, Harbottle (below), Holystone, Alwinton, Ingram and Kirknewton are the main villages in the National Park. Each has its own personality, based on chance or circumstance. In spring most verges are alive with daffodils and in summer the gardens are a riot of shrubs and hardy perennials. Hanging baskets and bright paintwork soften the austere stonework.

Northumberland farmhouses were built to withstand the worst weather. Grey sandstone walls, stone-slated roofs, solid lintels and small windows were the rule. Grouped around each square farmyard were usually a stable, byre, hemmel (shelter-shed) and perhaps a piggery and 'netty' (privy or outside toilet). Farmsteadings like this, at Low Old Shield, often date back to the end of the 18th century.

the shepherd's year

Breeding and rearing sheep is one of the main occupations of hill farmers. Until recently large tenant farms employed shepherds, who lived in cottages in the hills and spent most of their time among their sheep. Today many farms have reduced their workforce and any remaining shepherds live in the valleys or in nearby villages. For small family farms however, the routine has changed very little. Everyone is involved; sons and daughters shepherd their father's flocks, then pass the task on to their own children.

The main sheep breeds on the Northumberland hills are the Cheviot (white face, no horns), the blackface (black or mottled face, with horns) and the Swaledale (black face and white muzzle, with horns). Blackface and Swaledale ewes are crossed with Blue-faced Leicester tups (rams) to produce mule lambs which are sold on to lowland farms for fattening.

The farming year begins in early winter when the tups are driven onto the hills to run with the ewes. In severe weather, when snow covers any grass or heather, the sheep are given silage or hay, but for most of the time they fend for themselves. They have to be hardy to survive. In February ewes carrying twins or triplets are given extra food and brought down to better grass in the inbye fields close to the farm. Lambing takes place in April or May, or even June for the hardy breeds that stay out on the hills. July is shearing (or clipping) time; in August the lambs are 'speaned' or weaned. The best sheep are then prepared for the local Shepherds' Shows, the main social event of the year; in September and October the annual marts take place. The only really quiet time is in the middle of a mild winter.

Gwen Wallace on Molly,
shepherding on Fulhope Edge,
Coquetdale.

high hills

The well-defined massif of the Cheviot Hills began life as a volcano nearly 400 million years ago, spewing out lava and ash. Shortly afterwards there was an upwelling of magma or moulten rock beneath the surface. The lava cooled to form andesite and the magma formed granite. The rolling grassy Cheviot foothills owe their special qualities to the andesite, whilst the heather-capped tops of the highest hills, notably The Cheviot itself, are exposed granite.

Four valleys, the College, Harthope, Breamish and Coquet, each carrying a river and a narrow road, cut into the Cheviots on the English side of the Border. Access into the heart of the hills is easy, at least in summer. The College Valley (left), in the north of the Park, is notable for its tranquillity, sense of space and breathtaking views. The road beyond Hethpool is private but a few car permits are available each day from John Sale and Partners in Wooler.

The most popular Cheviot valley and a traditional picnic venue for Tynesiders, is the Breamish. A side road leads westwards from Powburn to the village of Ingram, which houses a National Park Centre in the old school. Above Ingram there are areas of level grassland (haughland) where cars can park alongside the river. For those feeling energetic, footpaths lead up to one of the finest historic landscapes in Britain, where every ridge and mound hides a secret. Archaeologists are only just beginning to appreciate the significance of this lonely place, where evidence of 4,000 years of hill farming lies undisturbed.

The Cheviots are great walking country. The Border Ridge marks the dramatic conclusion of the first and best-known of long distance paths, the Pennine Way. Walkers who began the 400kms (250 miles) National Trail at Edale in Derbyshire have a testing last lap of 43kms (27 miles) from Byrness to Kirk Yetholm. This stretch links a string of handsome hills from Beefstand to Windy Gyle (left) and The Schil. It used to be very boggy, but recent management work by the National Park Authority has transformed the route.

people and pastimes

Spare time used to be a precious commodity; it was valued and exploited. Television and easy communications, even in the remote valleys of the National Park, have smoothed away traditions. Yet there are still local sports played at the Shepherds' Shows and many arts and crafts that are learnt are developed in the quiet of the countryside.

The most respected skills around the Border villages are those associated with work, such as drystone walling. Walling is particularly difficult to do well, the results are in full view for everyone to judge. A ton of stone is used for every metre of wall and it takes a day to build three or four metres. Not surprisingly, wallers such as the Hall family (right) are strong, skilful characters, usually quiet and weatherbeaten.

Shepherds, who by tradition lead a lonely life, have a wide range of pastimes associated with their work. Dog breeding and trialling are popular and stick dressing, creating beautifully worked crooks or walking sticks usually out of rams horns and hazel shafts, is still a noted competition craft among shepherds like Peter Dixon (right).

Northumberland is one of the few regions in England with a distinctive musical tradition that has been passed from generation to generation and is still thriving. The border hills have produced some celebrated shepherd fiddlers such as Willie Taylor (below) and small-pipe players like the late Joe Hutton. The revival of folk / roots music has seen the Northumbrian tradition passed on through Alastair Anderson, Kathryn Tickell and Nancy Kerr. It is still possible to go to a village dance and be thrilled by an accordion band.

what's in a name?

Look at a map of the National Park and you will notice a host of unfamiliar words attached to place-names. Many are local to Northumberland and here is what some of them mean:

Bell – a hill
Birk or *Birks* – where birch trees grow
Burn – stream
Cairn – pile of stones
Cleugh – ravine
Dene – broad valley
Dyke – embankment (made from the digging of a ditch)
Eal – island or piece of floodable land
Flother – where water flows over swampy ground
Hagg – a bank of peat, or a place to shelter cattle
Haugh – flat land in a river valley
Heugh – a ridge which ends abruptly
Hirst – wood
Hope – strip of better land in a valley
Knowe – small hill or slope
Law – domed hill or mountain
Lee or *Lea* – clearing
Linn – waterfall
Moss – peat bog or mire
Rigg – ridge
Scar – bare or broken rock
Shank – a projecting point of a hill (like a shin-bone)
Shaw or *Shaws* – copse or small wood
Shiel or *Shield* – summering ground, or hut used during transhumance
Sike – small stream or rivulet
Tod – fox

An easy 2.5kms (1^1/$_2$ miles) walk following the Hareshaw Burn from Bellingham will bring you to Hareshaw Linn.

reiver country

The North Tyne, the home of otters, goosanders and sandpipers is the broadest and deepest river to flow through the National Park. Its headwaters have been dammed at Kielder and for most of the middle reach, from the dam wall near Falstone down to Bellingham bridge, it is steady, tree-lined and very pretty.

But despite its attractive river valley the reputation of Tynedale rests on treachery and murder. According to a 16th century survey the area was 'plenished with . . . wild and misdemeaned people'. These were the notorious Reivers or Moss Troopers, families who made the most of lawless times to ride against their neighbours, stealing anything they could carry and burning whatever was left. In the long centuries of on-off Border Wars life was held to be cheap; rustling cattle was the easiest way to fill the larder.

In such troubled times people had to defend themselves or starve. An act of 1555 had identified a twenty mile border zone in need of special protection. By the mid 17th century dozens of bastles (defensible farmhouses) had appeared in Tynedale, Redesdale and Coquetdale. These were far from picturesque structures. Their main features included massively thick walls and on the ground floor (used for storage) an absence of windows. When an attack was threatened the occupants barred the door, climbed a ladder to the upper floor, drew it up behind them, shut the trapdoor and hoped for the best.

The brute strength of the bastles is demonstrated by the fact that many have survived, in various stages of neglect and decay. The Reivers Trail, a joint National Park / Forest Enterprise project, follows a waymarked route to some of the most interesting bastles, notably Barty's Pele and Black Middens (left) in North Tynedale.

But many folk in Tynedale possessed nothing worth defending and left nothing to tell their tale. Their lives are recorded in old haymeadows, drystone walls and sheep stells (shelters).

The North Tyne near Ridley
Stokoe picnic site.

a battleground

Travelling along the A68 through Redesdale, it is hard to believe that this relatively peaceful valley has been the scene of much military activity over the last 2,000 years. Roman legions were here first. Their great highway Dere Street, guarded by High Rochester (right), the most northerly occupied fort in the Roman Empire, and bordered by temporary camps such as Chew Green, ran up the valley to its destination near Inverness.

In medieval times, Redesdale was no stranger to the ravages of war as England and Scotland battled for control of the Borders. One of the most celebrated encounters between English and Scottish armies took place near Otterburn (on the edge of the National Park) in 1388. Celebrated in a rousing ballad the battle, fought by moonlight, ended in defeat for the English. Percy's Cross stands near the spot where ironically the Scottish commander, the Early of Douglas, was killed. Henry Percy (Shakespeare's Harry Hotspur) who led the English, was captured, ransomed and lived to fight another day.

In the 15th and 16th centuries, the reiving families of Redesdale – Halls, Reeds, Hedleys, Potts, Dunns and Fletchers – were amongst the most notorious in the Borders; 'they do . . . delyte and use themselves in Theftes and spoyles'. Two hundred years of reiving had its effect on Redesdale. Because of the insecurity the land suffered and continued to be called 'waste' until more settled times in the 18th century.

Part of the 'waste' or wilderness of Redesdale is now in the Ministry of Defence Otterburn Training Area, which is wholly within the National Park. Access to the Training Area between Redesdale and Coquetdale is restricted because of live firing but the land north of the River Coquet is open at all times.

In the Upper Rede Valley, the A68 marks the boundary of the National Park. The road runs alongside Catcleugh Reservoir, built at the turn of the century by navvies from Newcastle and Gateshead. They and their families lived on site in wooden cabins, one of which has been restored by Northumbrian Water and the Park Authority as a visitor centre. A beautiful stained glass window in the tiny church at Byrness commemorates the men, women and children who died at Catcleugh all those years ago.

blackland

Only in the uplands of Britain can you see hillscapes awash with purple heather. The plant has very precise requirements; it thrives on wet moorland where there is no lime in the soil. For the last couple of centuries heather moorland on big estates has been and is being carefully managed for red grouse, and where grouse do well, so do many other birds and animals. In Northumberland most of the finest moors are to be found on the ridge of Fell Sandstone running in a great arc around the Cheviots. Outcrops of weathered sandstone, like Harbottle Crags (left), set in a sea of heather on the shoulders of the Coquet Valley, are among the most dramatic. It is possible to explore this area from car parks at Lordenshaws at the foot of Simonside, Darden in the Grasslees Valley and from Holystone, Harbottle and Alwinton.

In Northumberland heather-covered hills are called 'blackland' as opposed to grass-covered 'whiteland'. From April to early June the moors are still dark, but the wildlife is of great interest. Birds include wheatear and golden plover and you may catch a glimpse of a merlin or a blackcock. Impressive day-flying moths are on the wing too, such as the emperor, northern eggar and fox-moth.

The best time of year to take to the moors is in late July and August, when the heather is in flower. Apart from the glorious colour there is also the scent and the constant hum of bees. Hives are put out to harvest the nectar and the honey is sold at many local shops. Bumblebees, hoverflies, moths and bugs also make the most of the free food and help to pollinate the heather.

Secrets of Simonside

Below the Simonside Ridge is a magical patchwork of moorland called Lordenshaws. Near the car park are traces of 7,000 years of settlement. Ancient rock carvings (left), cairnfields, burial mounds and stone cists (coffins), the ramparts of a massive Iron Age hill fort and the boundary bank of a medieval deer park are all visible and accessible. A short drive west of Lordenshaws along the hillside road brings you to the massive ruins of Tosson Tower, a medieval tower house and further on, to the restored Tosson Limekiln and picnic area.

conservation

Successful conservation is usually invisible. Nothing stays the same, even in remote Northumberland. The essential task of the National Park Authority is to conserve a working landscape, to support a lively community whilst retaining or improving the qualities that attract people here.

Wildlife conservation involves the support of farmers. Non-intensive methods, which benefit the environment, are no longer the cheapest way to manage the land. The Park can help by giving advice and grants. Recent schemes have included moorland conservation by bracken control, revegetation of the Cheviot summit, rescue and management of mires and the planting of new native woodland. National Park Conservation Officers work closely with farmers and larger landowners such as Forest Enterprise and the MoD, The Duke of Northumberland, Lilburn Estates, College Valley Estates and the National Trust.

Buildings are important to the character of the landscape. The large number of listed buildings in the Park range from castles and bastles, such as Woodhouses (left), to farmhouses and limekilns. The Park Authority tries to conserve these and contributes to the preservation of other workaday structures that add interest to the countryside.

Archaeological features are of special value. Over the last few years the importance of prehistoric landscapes has been recognised and the Northumberland uplands are proving to be particularly exciting. Ancient monuments are scattered throughout the Park and in some places whole hillsides are studded with remains of long-lost farming systems. Conservation in this case is a matter of encouraging awareness and sensitive management, such as avoiding overstocking or damage of a site through deep ploughing or digging drainage channels. The key to successful conservation of archaeological sites often lies in management agreements between the National Park Authority and private landowners. So, when you look at an attractive landscape, like the hay meadow on the left, you are looking at conservation in action.

wide blue yonder

The Northumberland hills are getting closer all the time.
For most people, what was once a faraway landscape only attainable on
specially organised holidays, is now a short ride away. Trying to balance
the conflicting interests of conservation and access is another task of the
National Park Authority. It isn't usually a problem; without the interest
and involvement of the local population, farmers and visitors any
landscape conservation would be a pointless exercise.

Information about the Park, how the landscape works and what
opportunities there are for enjoying it, is available from publications,
leaflets and trails. The National Park's 'What's On' booket lists dozens of
special walks or events throughout the year, from family activities such as
pond-dipping and farm visits to map-reading, strenuous high hills
walking and winter bivouacs. Walks books provide full descriptions, maps
and along-the-way details about some of the best routes to take.

Informal contact, meeting Rangers or Voluntary Wardens out on the
hills, is how some people get to know about the work of the Park
Authority. Many other visitors call in at National Park Centres (at Once
Brewed, near Hadrian's Wall, Rothbury in Coquetdale and Ingram in the
Breamish Valley) or pick up a leaflet at a National Park Information Point,
local library or B&B. Those who live in nearby towns may be introduced
to the wide blue yonder through their children and the National Park's
Education Service. Whatever the initial contact, the best way to enjoy
Northumberland National Park is to explore it for yourself, to let it tell
you its own story.

Above Mount Hooley, on the
footpath to the Border Ridge,
with Newton Tors in the
background.

gazetteer

One of the pleasures of visiting an area of countryside that is new to you is to discover places of special interest, scenic and historic. This gazetteer is not a comprehensive guide to Northumberland National Park but rather an appetiser. It is intended to give visitors a taste of some of the treasures in store in this little known part of England and to encourage further exploration. The OS Leisure Series of maps covers most of the National Park. A comprehensive guide to public transport is available from Northumberland County Council (Tel. 01670 533128).

Key to symbols
Parking **P**   Toilets **WC**   Picnics ⊓   Walks 👣
Limited Public Transport / Post Bus 🚐

Alwinton NT 922064 The last village in Upper Coquetdale. A good starting point for walks on the Border Ridge. The big event of the year is the traditional Border Shepherd's Show held on the second Saturday in October which attracts many visitors from far and wide. **P WC** 👣 🚐

Bellingham NY 838835 The main village in North Tynedale. It hosts the local show – sheep judging, home produce competitions, displays and country crafts, on the last Saturday in August. Hareshaw Linn, a wooded valley with spectacular waterfall is on the outskirts of the village.

Breamish Valley NU 039169 High hills, a picturesque river setting and one of the most important archaeological landscapes in England. Many remains from Neolithic and Bronze Age burials to hillforts, farmsteads, field systems and deserted medieval villages. National Park Centre at Ingram NU 019164. **P WC** ⊓ 👣

Chew Green NT 788085 Roman military complex at the head of the Coquet Valley, accessible at all times. The series of superimposed temporary camps and fortlet are best viewed from a small layby on the opposite hill, Thirlmoor NT 795080. Check with the Otterburn Training Area Range Control Officer first (Tel. 01830 520569) in case live firing is taking place.

College Valley NT 90–30 Secluded, peaceful, unspoilt. For the more adventurous, Henhole and the Bizzle provide challenging ascents to the top of The Cheviot, Northumberland's highest hill at 815m (2,665 feet). The summit is long and flat. Neighbouring hills offer better views. Access from West Newton NT 904303. The road beyond Hethpool is private but some car permits are available each day from John Sale and Partners in Wooler (Tel. 01668 281611). **P** 👣

Elsdon NY 938938 Historic capital of Redesdale. It has a 14th century church where the dead from the Battle of Otterburn are reputedly buried, a fascinating churchyard, a medieval tower house (privately owned), the earthworks of a Norman motte and bailey castle and a large village green. **P WC** 👣 🚐

Falstone NY 125875 Of particular interest in this little village near Kielder Water in North Tynedale, are the elaborate Victorian drinking fountain and the early 18th century sculptured gravestones in the churchyard, including that of a girl holding hands with a skeleton. **P WC** ⊓ 🚐

Hadrian's Wall World Heritage Site NY 67-82 The most famous ancient monument in Northumberland is Hadrian's Wall, accessible by seasonal public transport. The central sector, most of which is owned by the National Trust, lies just inside the southern boundary of the National Park. Access is clearly signed from several places along the B6318. Places to visit include: **Housesteads** NY 790688 Dramatically sited Roman fort on the crags of the Whin Sill. Extensively excavated and consolidated – barracks, granaries, hospital, latrine and remains of a large civilian settlement outside the fort. **P WC** ⌐ 🚌

Once Brewed NY 753668 National Park Centre about 5kms west of Housesteads on the B6318. **P WC** ⌐ 🚌

Walltown NY 675663 Reclaimed quarry now a National Park recreation site with lake, pond and waymarked trails. Small information centre open seasonally. **P WC** ⌐ 🚌

Cawfields NY 713665 Another reclaimed quarry and National Park recreation site. Direct access to an interesting section of Hadrian's Wall and a milecastle. Excellent views of the vallum. **P WC** ⌐ 🚌

Greenlee Lough NY 770697 National Nature Reserve north of Hadrian's Wall. Access by foot only from Housesteads or Steel Rigg. Bird hide, boardwalk.

Harbottle NT 935046 One of the loveliest villages in Coquetdale. The single street of houses is overlooked by the ruins of a 12th century castle. A path leads up to the Drake Stone a massive Fell Sandstone boulder and to a glacial lough (lake) beyond. **P** 🔎 🚌

Harthope Valley NT 976250 A long, very pretty valley, a favourite with birdwatchers and walkers in summer. From Langleeford there is a steady climb up The Cheviot, Northumberland's highest hill 815m (2,665ft). **P** ⌐ 🔎 🚌

Holystone NT 955027. Tiny stone-built village. Main attraction is the Holy Well, traditionally the site of early Christian baptisms and the source of Holystone's water supply. Forest walks which include the Holystone Burn Nature Reserve, start at the car park a short distance out of the village. **P** 🔎 🚌

High Rochester NY 832986 A small hamlet in Redesdale, nestling within the ramparts of an outpost fort north of Hadrian's Wall. From the west gate the outline of a large Roman temporary camp can be seen on the far side of the Sills Burn. **P** 🔎

Kirknewton NT 914303 The village and its surrounds are in a National Park conservation area. In the church, the vaulted chancel and south transept are dramatic reminders of the dangers that existed on the Borders long ago. 🔎 🚌

Lordenshaws NZ 053988 Impressive remains of an Iron Age hillfort, Bronze Age burials and rock carvings in open heather moorland close to the forested slopes of the Simonside Hills. **P** 🔎 🚌

Otterburn Training Area: Occupies one fifth of the National Park in Redesdale and Coquetdale. North of the River Coquet the network of footpaths and bridleways is accessible at all times and is popular with hill walkers. When there is no firing in progress you are welcome to visit other parts of the Training Area to view some of the historic sites such as bastles. For reasons of safety you should always inform the Range Control Officer of your intended visit. (Tel. 01830 520569). Leaflets explaining access and places to visit can be picked up from National Park Centres and TIC's.

Rothbury NU 058016 Busy market town just outside the National Park. Popular with visitors. Good centre for gentle walks round about or for exploring the Simonside Hills and Upper Coquetdale. National Park Centre near the church.

Stonehaugh NY 789762 A village built in 1957 to house Forestry Commission workers. **P** ⌐ 🔎 🚌

Wooler NT 993280 Market town in Glendale. Gateway to the Cheviot Hills and the northern valleys of the National Park. Glendale Show, on the last Monday in August, a Bank Holiday, is well supported by holiday makers and locals.

call in and meet us

Northumberland National Park has three Centres where staff will help you plan your visit and tell you more about the area.

Each has exhibitions, videos to watch and a wide range of free leaflets and other information. They sell maps, books, National Park clothing and souvenirs.

Northumberland National Park Centre, Once Brewed
Hadrian's Wall,
Military Road,
Bardon Mill,
Northumberland
NE46 7AN
Tel. 01434 344396

Northumberland National Park Centre, Rothbury
Church House,
Church Street,
Rothbury,
Northumberland
NE65 7UP
Tel. 01669 620887

Northumberland National Park Centre, Ingram
Ingram,
Powburn,
Alnwick,
Northumberland
NE66 4LT
Tel. 01665 578248

The Centres are closed in the winter. Please contact National Park Headquarters for further information.

Front Cover: The College Valley
Forward: College Burn near Hare Law

Northumberland National Park
Eastburn
South Park
Hexham
Northumberland
NE46 1BS
Tel. 01434 605555

Northumberland National Park also operates a number of Information Points in cafes, shops and other businesses in and around the Park. Look out for the sign with the curlew. You can be sure of detailed local knowledge and a warm welcome.

acknowledgements

Text by Tony Hopkins
Gazetteer and Editing by Beryl Charlton
Photographs by Tony Hopkins. Additional photography by Eric Dale, Simon Fraser, Tim Gates, Julian Morrison-Bell, Graeme Peacock and The National Trust and National Park staff.
Map by Ann Rooke

Designed by Spring House Design Associates, Hexham

Northumberland
NATIONAL PARK

Produced and published by
Northumberland National Park Authority
Eastburn, South Park, Hexham, Northumberland, NE46 1BS
© Northumberland National Park Authority 1997

Printed by Studio Print on environmentally friendly paper.